Orchid Care for Beginners

Your Complete Beginner's Guide to Cultivating Stunning Orchids at Home

By: Lily Greenwood

Table of Contents

Starting your Orchid Journey..1

    Orchid Selection: How to Select your First Orchid..................4

    Home at last, now what? 6

        Growing Requirement for Orchids-Light 7

        Growing Requirement for Orchids-Soil and Drainage 8

        Growing Requirement for Orchids- Art of Watering 12

        Growing Requirement for Orchids-Temperature and Humidity 13

        How to Properly Deal with a Hungry Orchid 14

A Beginner's Guide to Potting and Repotting an Orchid ...19

A General Guide on Orchid Propagation 23

        How to Propagate Phalaenopsis Orchids............................24

        How to Propagate Cattleya Orchids 26

        Moving your Orchid to a New Home (Transplanting) 30

        Not Just another Pot-How to Plant a Mounted Orchid 31

Common Pests and Plant Diseases of Orchids 37

        Common Pests that Attack Orchids....................................39

        Common Plant Diseases of Orchids....................................49

        Bacterial Issues of Orchids..49

        Fungal Issues of Orchids..49

        Viral Issues of Orchids 50

Which Orchid Should I Start With?...51

Creating an Orchid Collection 57

Plants to Avoid at an Orchid Show 58

V is for Vanilla...61

Care of the Vanilla Orchid 63

orchid is healthy or not. A healthy orchid's roots will feel plump when touched. They will also be white or green. On the other hand, a root that feels squishy and is brown or black is an indication that the plant is sick.

If you cannot see the roots clearly, be bold and remove the plant from its decorative container. This inner container is called a grower pot, and it is used because it has drainage.

The following structure to look at on the orchids is the leaves. If a plant has all yellow leaves, then leave it at the store. On the other hand, if the bottom leaf is yellow, well, this is normal as long as the top leaves are green. The reason for the yellow leaves on the bottom in this example is age. As leaves mature, their ability to do their job correctly is diminished. Time causes them to turn yellow, but as the natural process goes on, newer and more efficient green leaves will be produced.

What if the leaves are green with yellow spots? If you see yellow spots on leaves, then you have an insect issue. To double-check this, though, make sure to look on the top and underneath each leaf for webs and white bumps. Both of these are signs of mealy bug or spider mite issues. If you find any of these symptoms, leave the orchid plant behind.

Once you have looked at the roots and leaves, the next characteristic to look at is the flowers. The orchid you are thinking about purchasing should be full of flowers that look healthy. They should also be tightly attached to the stem. To extend the enjoyment of your orchid, try to find one where only some of the blooms have opened.

As it is essential to have a strong and healthy root system to hold the plant up, the blooms need a sturdy spike to support the flowers. Orchid flowers are lightweight, but when you get a group of them, they are a bit weighty. Without the proper support, your orchid flowers will come tumbling down onto the table. So, what do you look for in an orchid spike? A healthy and supportive orchid stem will be tall and have a slight arch to it where the blooms/flowers are located. If you find that the spike appears to be buckling under the weight, then do not purchase this plant. A weak spike is an indication of an unhealthy plant.

The last trait to check off the list is smell. Yes, you read that correctly. Your nose can help you determine if the plant is healthy or not. So, what does a healthy orchid smell like? Well, the most straightforward answer is to describe what type of aroma an unhealthy orchid produces. If you describe the smell as a foul or musty smell, then you need to walk away from this plant. This simple smell is an indication of rotting plant material, which is not a positive thing.

Home at last, now what?

When it comes to orchid care, there are five requirements: light, soil/drainage, watering, temperature/humidity, and fertilizing. While all these requirements can be overwhelming, let's break them down into easy-to-digest parts.

Grocery store orchids are in two pots. The first pot is a decorative element. It can be made of clay or plastic and usually does not have a drainage hole. On the other hand, the inner pot or liner is generally made of plastic and should have at least one drainage hole in the bottom. This is not enough, but we will get back to that issue in a minute.

Orchids bought at a plant nursery are typically sold in one container, which has at least one drainage hole in the bottom.

Why the difference in packaging? Well, a grocery store views the purchase of an orchid as a quick gift. The present would look shabby if it were in the liner pot. On the other hand, orchids bought at plant nurseries are not necessarily being purchased that day as a gift, which would give the owner of the plant time to select a decorative container.

While we will talk about pots later, the point to make now is that drainage is essential not only when it comes to potting medium but also the pots that house orchids. If you find that the pot that contains the roots of your orchid has one drainage hole, it is recommended to make additional holes in the bottom and along the sides of the container so that there are enough openings by which water can drain. This can quickly be done with the plant in the pot with an ice pick or the pointy tip of a pair of scissors. Do not heat the ice pick tip as an example to create the holes. As long as the orchid is still in the inner pot, it is a good idea not to use heat.

Before you start making holes haphazardly, there is a simple formula to follow when creating additional drainage holes in your inner container. If your inner pot is three to four inches in diameter, you will need four to eight drainage holes. For inner pots that are five to six inches in diameter, eight to twelve holes will be required.

Growing Requirement for Orchids- Art of Watering

Because of the location where wild orchids grow, you may think that special water is required for these plants. The answer is yes, and no. Regular tap water is fine as long as it is lukewarm to room temperature and is not softened with salt.

How often to water your orchid is the next question many indoor gardeners have. The rule is to allow the planting medium

The second fertilizing exception concerns your orchid's blooming stage. Once your plant starts forming blooms, stop fertilizing until the flowers are spent or finished. The blooming of any plant indicates that conditions are right. Continuing to fertilize during this time is a waste of money and time because the plant will simply not be using the nutrients.

Another point to make when it comes to feeding your orchid has to do with micronutrients. Just like humans, plants have macro and micronutrient requirements. The prepackaged orchid fertilizer will provide the macronutrients, and fish emulsion or seaweed extract will supply the micronutrients. However, micronutrients will not be utilized as liquid fertilizers. Instead, one will need to mist their orchid with either of the ingredients mentioned.

The frequency of misting is once a month due to the amount of these nutrients required by the orchid.

A General Guide on Orchid Propagation

As a beginning orchid gardener, propagating an orchid from seed can be difficult. Even seasoned orchid growers find growing orchids from seeds extremely challenging. The reason for this is the fact that the orchid seed's ability to be successful is directly tied to its environment. In the wild, the seed would fall in an area with hopes that a particular fungus would be available. This fungus would enter the orchid's root system and convert nutrients into a form that the roots could use. Yes, this is very different compared to other seeds. The reason is that other seeds have a natural storage system for nutrients that carry the seed and seedling until it can start making its food. Without this storage system, orchid seeds are dependent on the fungus for food. This is why orchids are very seldom grown from seed.

While the fungus is the main reason orchids are not grown from seed, the other reason is the amount of time. It takes months before you see any evidence of growth, and at that, it requires a magnifying glass. If you are lucky enough to get a seed to germinate, well, you are looking at three to eight years before the plant blooms for the first time.

Another way of propagating orchids is through division. Now, regardless of the division type, no orchid should be repotted, transplanted, or divided while it is actively flowering. Since there are only two types of orchids recommended for beginners, we will take a look at each one and learn their particular propagation techniques.

How to Propagate Phalaenopsis Orchids

To understand the propagation method, we must first understand this type of orchid. Phalaenopsis are known to produce offshoots or keikis, which is a Hawaiian word meaning "baby" or "child." These offshoots are produced along an orchid's nodes and are encouraged to form by the accumulation of a growth hormone.

This type of orchid tends to grow upward versus spreading along the ground. In doing so, you can find these keikis forming along the "stem" of the orchid. These offshoots will have their own leaves and roots and can even bloom.

Some orchid growers believe in keeping the keikis and mother plant together because removing a keikis will delay it's blooming again by two to three years. On the other hand, eliminating the offshoots or some of the offshoots will not affect the mother plant's ability to bloom again.

If your Phalaenopsis orchid has some offshoots, do not jump into dividing the plant. First, you will need to make sure that the plant is done flowering. Second, you will need to make sure that the offshoot has roots, and third, you will need to make sure they are long enough. Yes, the origins of your keikis need to be a certain length. What is the size? Well, the roots need to be two to three inches, and your keikis need to have at least three roots.

Once you have determined that your offshoot is big enough to remove, the next step is to sterilize everything. Why? Well, the reason goes beyond a clean pot. Anything you are going to cut with will need to be sterilized after every cut, and the cut(s) do not pre-moisten this material. Depending on what type of orchid you are working with, you do not automatically cut off the spent flower stalk.

Now that the general particulars are in order let's discuss the steps to rehoming your orchid plant.

Since you are rehoming your orchid to add a new planting medium, the first step is to fill a bucket halfway with cool water. Next, place your planted orchid in the water for 12 to 15 minutes. This will make it easier to remove the orchid from the pot and to remove the old orchid soil from the plant's roots.

After the soak, take the container out of the water and remove the orchid. Place the plant on the workspace. Utilizing the bucket, dump out the water and refill it with hot water along with a squirt of dish soap and a capful of bleach. Place the pot in this solution and allow it to soak for a few minutes. Scrub the inside to remove any debris. Rinse with warm water and set out to dry. While the pot is drying, gently work with the roots to remove as much of the spent potting medium as possible. Remove any dead or diseased roots along with any yellowing leaves with pruners that have been sterilized with rubbing alcohol.

At this point, you are ready to repot using a fresh planting medium. While the process is easy, it starts with the pot that you have washed. The inside of the container must be dry. If it still appears to be a bit damp, wipe it out with a paper towel. Next, place a small amount of orchid potting mix in the bottom of the container. Now, you are ready to put your orchid plant back into its pot. When doing this, make sure that you have all the roots inside the container. The next step is to start adding a potting medium around the roots. To really work the potting medium down through the container, gently tap the bottom of the pot on a hard surface. Continue to add the potting medium until you reach the lower leaves. Do not try to force the crown of the orchid deep into the planting medium. It should be slightly set above the planting medium with some of the roots exposed.

The last step is to perform a process called "watering in." This technique involves watering your plant so that the soil can settle around the roots.

Beyond rehoming, you will also want to clean your orchid. This concept may sound strange, but orchid leaves get dusty. In the wild, the orchid plant is exposed to rain, which will naturally wash its leaves. But, when grown indoors, this natural service is only available if you create it. At the same time, your first thought may be placing your orchid in the shower to mimic rain. This is not required and can easily cause damage to your orchid. On the other hand, gently misting your orchid is not going to clean the leaves. The best approach for cleaning the leaves of an orchid is to use a soft, moist cloth and wipe them down once a week.

Moving your Orchid to a New Home (Transplanting)

Before moving on, let's discuss the difference between rehoming and transplanting. Rehoming involves adding completely new soil to the roots but putting the orchid back into the same pot.

Transplanting, on the other hand, requires that the orchid be replanted into a different pot.

Now, some beginning gardeners may feel that the more enormous container you go to, the less you will have to transplant. There are a few things that could be improved with that idea. In general, placing any plant in a container that is too big will cause a lot of root growth but less growth above ground. To encourage equal growth of roots and foliage, the rule is to upsize one to two inches and no more. For example, if your orchid is in a four-inch pot, it can be transplanted into a six-inch container.

Beyond the container size, rehoming and transplanting processes are the same. Just remember that when transplanting, you will need to remove as much of the old planting medium as possible and utilize fresh material only in the pot.

Not Just another Pot-How to Plant a Mounted Orchid

The term "mounting orchids" is a form of transplanting where you mount or plant your orchid on a slab of wood. In actuality, this is how nature intended orchids to grow, free in the trees and branches so their long, plump roots could extend through the space, not be confined by a pot. Another reason to consider mounting your orchid is the fact that the flower stalk does not need to be staked. This will enhance the beauty of your orchid because it will allow it to shine as Mother Nature intended.

Displaying your orchid in this format not only opens up numerous ways by which you can display your plant. Now, your orchid can be displayed on a tabletop or hung on a wall. The other advantage of utilizing vertical space for your orchids is the fact that it frees up space on tables for more orchids.

As the saying goes, for every pro, there is a con, and this is true for mounted orchids. The pro of this approach is that a mounted orchid does not have to be transplanted as often as a potted orchid. The con of mounted orchids comes down to watering. Orchids displayed in this fashion require watering more often than the potted version. This extra hydration can be daily versus once a week for container-growing orchids.

Hardwood tree branches are an excellent source of mounting material. This includes sassafras, white oak, highbush blueberry, dogwood, and mesquite. Some fruit tree branches can also be used, including citrus, cherry, and persimmon. Beyond this, you can use redwood, cedar, cork bark, mopani, tree fern slabs, and mounting kits.

Other materials you will need include coconut fiber, sphagnum moss, rigid wire, wire snips, needle-nose pliers, an electric drill, and fishing line.

The first step in mounting is to study your piece of wood and determine whether you are going to hang it or display it on a table. Once you have chosen the answer, drill a hole in the wood and thread a wire through the hole. Next, shorten the wire as needed and create a loop by twisting the wire together.

To prepare your orchid for mounting, you will first soak your orchid's roots for about 20 minutes. Next, gently remove the old potting medium from around the roots of the plant. Cut away any dead roots and dispose of them in the trash.

While your orchid's roots are soaking, place a good amount of sphagnum moss or coconut fiber in a bucket of water. Allow this to soak for 20 minutes. After 20 minutes, you will first create a moisture pad for your orchid by taking moistened moss or fiber, squeezing out the excess water, and securing it to your mounting wood by wrapping the fishing line around the board and moss or fiber.

Next, spread the roots of your orchid around the wood slab and cover them with moistened moss or fiber. Secure everything together by wrapping the fishing line around your orchid's roots and the slab. During this process, make sure that the fishing line does not cut into the roots.

Watering a mounted orchid can be a bit challenging, but the easiest way is to take it down. Once that is done, move it to the sink and gently water the roots. Before returning your orchid to its honorable spot, make sure that all the excess water has drained away. This will prevent any damage to walls and/or floors from dripping water.

To Stake an Orchid or Not to Stake That is the Question

Without being overdramatic, the question is often asked whether an orchid needs to be staked. Before moving on, though, one item needs to be made clear. The staking refers to the flower stalk, not the stem.

Today, blooming orchids will be found with stakes. This makes sense, or does it? Orchids in the wild do not have stakes to hold their flower stalks, and they seem to do fine, right? Well, in truth, orchids growing in the tropical rainforest have natural supports. Some orchids grow on trees that use the branches to support not only themselves but their blooms. Other orchids nest themselves among other plants, which provide that support naturally. But, orchids that we have displayed in our homes need to have these environmental options. In doing so, they depend on us to provide that support, which is rewarded by their beautiful display of blooms and flowers.

When it comes to displaying, staking actually helps with the showboating of the flower stalk. How would staking make the blooms on an orchid more beautiful? Well, staking does two things. One, it reduces the chances of the flower stalk breaking, which will cause your gorgeous flowers to come tumbling to their death. The second purpose of staking is to provide support so that you can bend the flower stalk to your liking. Yes, I said, bending. Now, before going on, keep in mind that you are not going to be able to create a whole new shape or unique bend in the flexible flower stalk. Instead, staking can give the gardener some freedom to help the orchid show off its best assets.

Before moving on with the staking topic, let's discuss a particular term used for the "flowering part "of an orchid. This is biologically called inflorescence. When talking about the flower stalk, we will utilize the term inflorescence.

The term staking refers to utilizing a rigid stick to provide support for the orchid inflorescence. This can be galvanized metal wire of different gauges or as simple as a bamboo pole. The positive aspect of using galvanized wire is the fact that it can be bent. This is especially important when it comes to Cattleya orchids due to the pseudobulbs. When staking this type of orchid, it is essential not to put the stake near a pseudobulb. Utilizing a material that can bend is an excellent way of working around the pseudobulbs during the staking process.

Another pro for using galvanized wire is that some companies have created commercial supports made of this wire, plus clips that can be attached to the top of the pot. At first, one may think that this wire plus clip product is just a marketing strategy, but it is not. Sometimes, pseudobulbs can make an orchid top-heavy. Combine this with an orchid inflorescence, and you will have a good chance of the orchid being pulled out of its pot. Utilizing the wire plus clip product creates an anchor for the top-heavy orchid while being flexible so that the inflorescence can easily be reached without damaging the pseudobulbs.

Bamboo is an excellent choice for staking Phalaenopsis inflorescence. It is strong enough to support the blooms/flowers and adds a natural-looking, decorative touch.

Staking cannot occur without fasteners that hold the plant material to the stake. Currently, green or brown twist ties and plastic "dragonfly" clips are the most popular. Floral tape is another type of fastener that will also aid in the bending or shaping of the galvanized wire and orchid inflorescence.

There really is no right or wrong way of staking once you have the support in the pot. There are two rules, though, when it comes to creating the support for your inflorescence. One, be careful when bending the flower stalk. Two, take your time when trying to manipulate the inflorescence. Quick and careless movements can destroy blooms and flowers, along with simply breaking off the spike.

When staking the Moth Orchid, the key is to start when the inflorescence is six to twelve inches tall. If you want to create an arching, shingled inflorescence, you will need to place the first tie one to inches below the first bud. Do not cut the stake until the inflorescence has reached its maximum height.

Staking of the Corsage Orchid should be started when the blooms begin to twist from their upside-down arrangement.

In both orchid examples, the manipulation of the flower stalk should be so that the flowers are in the best position to show off their beauty.

Now, the question always comes up as to if and when you remove the staking/support. In the case of the Moth Orchid, it is OK to leave it due to the fact that the existing flower spike will flower again. On the other hand, the Corsage Orchid will only flower once on that spike. In doing so, remove the stake and spike when the flowers on this orchid are done blooming.

Common Pests and Plant Diseases of Orchids

Regardless of how careful an indoor gardener you are, there will be a time that you have to deal with a pest and/or plant disease problem. When it comes to orchids, these little beauties can attract an assortment of pests and diseases when they are planted outside. On the other hand, they are not immune to these problems just because they are grown indoors. The following information will give you a guide and solution to the most common pests and plant diseases that can be found on orchids. But before jumping in, the key to reducing the damage of pests and/or diseases is to know your orchids and listen to what they say. Believe it or not, they will provide you with clues as to what is going on. There is a catch, though, and it requires you to get to know your orchids personally.

Why do I bring this up? Orchids are slow growers, which means that some diseases can move in very quickly, and once the problem is crystal clear, it may be too late to save the plant. Another way to look at it, though, is since they are slow growers, this gives the gardener time to get to know their plants and pick up differences quicker compared to fast-growing plants. Regardless of whether you consider their slow growth as a blessing or a curse, it does give you time to observe and enjoy their growth.

Another issue arises when trying to diagnose a plant's response to a pest or disease. Unfortunately, some symptoms of pests and/or diseases are common to several issues. Two misdiagnosed issues that one faces when raising orchids are cultural problems, which are neither pests nor diseases, but their symptoms can mimic other plant problems.

The first one appears as shriveled and dry leaves. Now, you may think that this symptom is due to underwatering, which is a possibility, but overwatering is also a possibility. Either under-or-overwatering causes the roots of the orchid not to be able to take up sufficient water.

Now, the first thing to consider is the underwatering aspect. This can be caused by just not watering enough and allowing the planting medium to dry out. Another cause can be not using enough planting medium. This can be a typical problem for orchids displayed on wood with a small amount of growing medium around their roots.

The solutions to these problems are to water more often, add more planting medium, and/or place your orchid in a different type of container.

Overwatering affects not only the leaves but also the roots. In this condition, the roots will be in poor condition and/or absent. The unhealthy roots can be brought on by overwatering, which will then make the orchid water-starved because the roots cannot take up water. Another cause of overwatering is the old planting medium, which is compacted around the roots.

The solution to this problem requires a few steps. The first one entails removing the orchid from its present container. Gently remove the spent soil from the roots. While you are doing this, remove any dead or soft roots using sterilized pruners. Once that is done, replant your orchid in a sterilized pot with fresh orchid oil.

In both situations described above, it is a good idea to remove shriveled-up or brown leaves with sterilized pruners.

Another common problem for orchids is heat stress. Shriveled leaves, bleached leaves, and sunburn are examples of this. It is generally caused by overexposure to sunlight.

If you feel that your plant is heat-stressed but is not showing signs, there is a simple test you can do before damage occurs. This must be done on a sunny day and begins by placing a leaf in your hand. If the leaf is warmer than your hand, then you move your orchid or provide it with more shade.

Common Pests that Attack Orchids

Mealy bugs and Scale

When it comes to orchids, the most common pest is mealybugs. Now, one cannot talk about mealybugs without including Scale. Both of these pests are hard to control. One reason for this is the fact that not only will mealybugs be on the plant, but they can also be in the planting medium. The best approach to dealing with this problem is to act as soon as you see the signs. But what are the signs of mealybugs and/or Scale? If you see cottony masses with sticky honeydew, then you have mealybugs and/or Scale. Now, what is honeydew? This substance is a sugary waste product produced by different sap-sucking insects, which include mealybugs and Scale.

What can you do if you find these pests on your orchids? If there are a few, one can start by cleaning the leaves with rubbing alcohol. You will then want to follow this treatment with several rounds of insecticides, which include Neem, horticultural oil, or insecticidal soap. Keep in mind that treating mealybugs and/or Scale takes diligence. If the pest gets out of hand, it is advised to throw the plant away to keep the pest from spreading to other plants.

Aphids and Ants

Aphids are common in orchids and are related to Scale. They are soft-bodied insects that move slowly over plant material. These insects are only about 1/8 inch in size, with a soft, pear-shaped body, long legs, antenna, and mouth parts that are designed for sucking. They can be green, black, or white. Aphids, by nature, are wingless, but females will give birth to winged aphids when the colony becomes too large. This adaptation provides aphids with the ability to infest on other plants quickly.

There are several symptoms to look for when it comes to aphids. One major hint that you have an aphid problem comes from the appearance of stunted growth, curled and/or distorted leaves, and overall poor growth. All of this is due to the fact that the aphids are "sucking the life" out of the plant.

To find aphids on your orchids, take a look at the new growth at the base of buds, on flowers, and the underside of leaves. Another area to look at is on the top of the leaves. Developing aphids shed white skins that they leave on the top of leaves. While many of the signs mentioned can lead to a determination that you have an aphid infestation, one of the most accessible signs to follow is the trail of white skins.

The second sign that is a clear indication that you have an aphid problem is two-fold. First is the appearance of honeydew, and the second is ants. Honeydew is a sweet substance that is produced as aphids eat. These little insects cannot digest all the plant juices that they suck out. In doing so, they excrete the excess, which ends up on the leaves and stems of the plant. Then, sooty mould is attracted to this excretion. Sooty mould is a fungus that, when present, makes the leaves and stems appear dirty and black. But sooty mould is not the only thing that is attracted to honeydew; ants love this substance and will defend it. They will also protect and care for the aphids that have been involved in its production. To increase the output of the sugary substance, ants will transport aphids to other plants so that they can continue with honeydew manufacturing. However, as the aphids move from plant to plant, they also possibly carry different viruses and diseases along with them.

Prevention is the best approach and begins with an inspection of any plant you plan on bringing into your indoor environment. If you have already noticed some damage and/or honeydew, the next best step is to control the ants. Keep in mind, though, that there needs to be more than one treatment-and-done approach. You will need to put out sugar-based ant baits and wait for seven-to-10 days. This is enough time to kill worker ants, but you will need to destroy the whole colony. For this reason, you will want to place new ant bait every seven to 10 days until you no longer see any ants.

Whiteflies

This pest is very similar to the aphid in that they are sucking insects. They also produce honeydew, which attracts ants who love the sweet treat. Just like the aphids, the ants will move whiteflies from one plant to another to keep the supply of honeydew available. Beyond this issue, whiteflies' eggs have an incubation period of 12 days. These eggs can be found on the underside of the leaves. Once the eggs have hatched, the nymphs crawl on the leaves and begin to suck. They will continue to mottle and feed for six weeks. At this point, they turn into four-winged adults that can live one to two months.

Now, the problem with this pest is that by the time you notice something, it may be too late. Orchids with a whitefly infestation will fail to thrive. New growth will show up as damaged and/or unhealthy. The leaves can develop a yellow-mottled appearance that leads to leaf loss. As with the aphids, sooty mold will appear, causing the orchid not to be able to perform photosynthesis in the affected areas, which will weaken the plant.

Prevention is the best approach, and it starts with keeping the area clean. While cleanliness is essential, it is also just as important to quarantine any new plant in the area for at least two weeks. To aid in early detection, set out yellow sticky cards to catch any pests before they become a big problem.

If you have a whitefly problem, the first thing you should do is kill the ants. Several commercial ant traps and baits can be used to kill the ants, but keep in mind that this will need to be done several times to eliminate the ant colony.

Mites

Mites are tiny insects that are difficult to see, but there are a few tricks one can use to determine if mites are attacking your orchids. The first question to ask yourself is if the underside of your orchid's leaves has a silvery appearance. If the answer is yes, then there is a good chance that you have a mite issue.

Does the top of your orchid's leaves have yellow spots that gradually turn brown? If the answer is yes, then you may have a mite problem. Are there silken webs hanging from the underside of the leaves? Well, if the answer is yes, then you could have a mite crisis. To complicate the issue, not all mites spin webs, as in the case of the false spider mite. But do not fret. There are two ways to tell if you have a mite infestation, which will clearly tell you if you have a mite invasion.

The first technique utilizes a plain, white piece of cloth, which you will use to wipe the top and underneath sections of each leaf. Once that is done, take a look at the fabric. If it is clean, then you do not have a mite issue. On the other hand, if you see reddish or brown streaks on the cloth, then you have a problem.

The second method requires a piece of white paper and a magnifying glass. To perform this test, hold the white paper under a leaf and gently shake it. Next, look at the paper to see if anything is moving. If you are having a hard time seeing what is on the paper, pull out a magnifying glass to aid in your search.

While mites are small, the damage they can cause can be enormous. First, mites disfigure the plant by sucking out sap and chlorophyll. The removal of chlorophyll is what gives the leaf a silvery appearance. Second, the drinking of the orchid's sap causes a bruising appearance on the flowers. Beyond these problems, mites can bring with them plant diseases.

Before moving on to control, let's take a look at the mite's lifecycle. A female will lay one large egg at a time. When this egg hatches, the mite is considered a nymph. This nymph will molten several times before it becomes an adult. Then, the process happens all over again.

This process is sped up with warmer temperatures, and at high temperatures, mites can go from egg to adult in one week. As the colony of mites grows, winged types are born so that they can fly to other plants.

During the autumn, the female will begin to lay a few eggs that contain males. The reason for this is so that the females can be fertilized and eggs deposited to produce the next season's offspring.

The first line of defense against mites is a three-fold approach. First, the problem can be prevented by increasing humidity. Why does this help? Mites consume sap from orchids, which have a high water content. It is easier to remove the excess water in a dry environment compared to one with high humidity. Increasing the humidity level is quickly done with a humidity tray.

Beyond humidity, you must keep your plant strong. This means understanding what your type of orchid requires in terms of the proper amount of light, watering, and fertilizing.

The second approach has to do with sanitation of the environment. One needs to remove all spent plant material and old potting medium, which can create hiding places for mites. While you are cleaning up the space, inspect your orchid for problems. Frequent plant inspection is the last approach and the one that is least used. It is easier to get control of a problem in the early stages. This is why plant inspection is essential in any pest management program.

What if you find mites on your orchid? The first step is to raise the humidity. Next, gently wash the orchid's foliage and then go back over each leaf with a soft towel. This will reduce the number of mites, but this is just a temporary fix.

Yes, there are miticides on the market, but you can make one that is just as good as the commercial kind, and it only takes a few ingredients. To make the DIY version, grab a pint of 409 household cleaner and a pint of rubbing alcohol. Add these ingredients to a gallon-sized spray container and top off with water. Spray the whole plant, making sure to hit the underside of each leaf. Repeat this process every three to four days until you have completed six to eight applications. Following this application process will ensure that both the adults and young are killed.

If this is too much trouble, consider placing your orchid outside if the weather is conducive to indoor plants. While you could be exposing your orchid to other issues, it allows natural predators to feed on the mites. One word of caution, though, when it comes to using nature to take care of a mite: Do not combine this with any form of chemical control. Doing this dual control method will kill not only the mites but also the predators that feed on them.

Cockroaches

Before moving on with these creepy crawlies, let's first clear a fact up. While cockroaches are known to be a problem for orchids that are placed outdoors in pots, they can also be a problem for indoor orchids. Before you get defensive over this matter, let's take a look at how cockroaches can get into your orchids.

First, cockroaches enter your potted orchids through the drainage hole at the bottom, even if your indoor orchids are displayed in an outer pot. These little guys will find a way into the potting medium. While you may not see them since they are nocturnal feeders, you will see the damage on your orchid if you know what to look for. When inspecting your orchid, take a look at the roots, new growth, and flowers. If these areas have been nibbled on, then you have a cockroach problem in the planting medium.

Prevention is the best step. This means sealing up any cracks in your home. Make sure that no food or water sources are available. This means no pet food is left out for man or beast, nor should you have any bowls of water out for your pets. You will also want to make sure that no faucets are dripping, which could provide a water source for this pest.

Next, if you did take your orchids out during the summer, make sure to submerge the pots in water. This will flush out the roaches from the planting medium before you take your plants in for the season.

Regardless of whether you took your orchids outside or not, you may find damage later on in the growing season. If this is the case, there are a few simple things you can do. One is to place sticky traps around the plants. Roaches are known to eat dead roaches, which will attract more. Another approach is to put a pan of equal parts baking soda and sugar around where you see evidence of roaches. This is a non-toxic version that will not hurt pets, but you could attract ants to the area.

If you see roaches on the top of the planting medium, there is another technique that one can use. You will need a few empty medicine bottles, school glue, and boric tablets. Remove the lid from the medicine bottles, place a few drops of school glue in the bottom of the bottles, and top with a few boric acid tablets. Allow the glue to dry. Once that has happened, lay the medicine bottles horizontally on the soil surface. At this point, the roaches will find the little containers tasty. The consumption of boric acid will address your cockroach problem.

Fungal Gnats

This is a widespread pest in orchids, and these little creatures do not cause plant damage. But, if you have them, you know how much of a pain they are. Before we move on to how to control these nuisances, let's take a look at what causes them in the first place.

In the wild, orchids do not attract fungal gnats. Why, you may be wondering? Well, it has to do with our domestication indoors. In the wild, the growing medium may or may not be covering the roots. While this sounds harsh and unbelievable, the wild orchid has adapted to a harsh environment where they survive in a well-draining medium. The domesticated climate is different. Here, orchid growers feed their plants with the best fertilizer and water them to death sometimes. No, this is not a deliberate act on the grower's part, but where nature removes and adds planting medium, the orchid grower does not or not as often as required. In doing so, the planting medium breaks down. This starts a cycle in the planting medium where the drainage of excess water is reduced, which leads to soggy soil and fungal gnats.

Now, since these little pests do not feed on the plant, what do they consume? As the name implies, it is a fungus that these little creatures desire, but that is not all. The larvae of the gnats feast on fungus growing in wet soil, especially old soil. The larvae of this gnat will then feed on dead plant material and sometimes very young roots of orchids. This latter food source, though, is uncommon.

Beyond changing the planting medium so that there are no eggs or fungus available, what else can be done? Fungal gnats are easy to catch in yellow sticky cards that are sold to catch aphids. If you see these little pests walking around on the soil surface, consider cutting some of the cards into strips and laying them on the soil surface. This latter approach is excellent for catching females since it is not common for them to fly.

Common Plant Diseases of Orchids

There are three types of plant diseases of orchids: bacterial, fungal, and viral. While particular species will not be mentioned, it is essential to understand the signs present for each. Once you understand how to read the signs, you will then know how to deal with the problem.

Bacterial Issues of Orchids

When it comes to diagnosing a bacterial issue, there are two techniques: the eyes and the nose. Spotted or recessed areas on the leaves represent a bacterial issue. This is caused by water sitting on the leaf, which creates the perfect environment for plant disease. The second way to tell if your orchid has a bacterial problem is through the aroma it produces. Soil that is too wet will have a foul smell, which is the ideal breeding ground for bacteria.

Fungal Issues of Orchids

Fungal problems show up in your orchid, such as rotting roots, rhizomes, and pseudobulbs. Spots on leaves can also be an indication of a fungal problem, while the latter is also an indication of a bacterial problem. But do not worry if you cannot tell the difference when your orchid leaves are spotted. The steps to dealing with either issue are the same but with a few differences.

Regardless of which problem you diagnose, the first step is to sterilize pruning shears with rubbing alcohol. Once that is completed, cut away the affected area. Now, this may take some time because you will need to wipe down the pruning shears every time you cut away infected material.

After you have removed all the infected areas, treat the wound with ground cinnamon mixed with white glue. Applying this mixture will seal up the area while it is healing and provide an antibacterial and antifungal treatment to keep the wound clean. This will prevent any other plant disease from taking up residence in the open wound.

Beyond this, clean and sterilize the environment to kill any lingering bacteria and fungus.

While these approaches will treat the problem, the best defense is to prevent the issue from happening in the first place. The first line of defense is to keep the area dry by utilizing a fan to move air around. This simple step helps in the evaporation of water on and around plants. The second defensive approach is to make sure that you always use sterilized pots and tools whenever you are working with your orchids. Finally, try not to overwater. Remember that wet soil is a welcoming invitation to any bacteria and fungi in the environment.

Viral Issues of Orchids

Viruses are more challenging to diagnose when compared to bacteria and fungi. Why, you may be wondering? Well, it all has to do with where these three disease types exist on the plant.

Bacteria and fungus grow on the plant while a virus is inside the plant. Having said that, though, plants with viral issues do show symptoms, and the most prominent symptom is color streaking. This is usually seen as color breaks in blooms, but to get a precise diagnosis, one needs to take a sample of tissue that is sent to a lab for testing.

Now, how does a virus get inside the orchid? Well, it all comes down to pests. Insects that suck sap out of an infected orchid will transfer some of that sap to another orchid. Hence, the virus is now in the tissue. But what can one do? The most crucial step is to prevent insect infestation by keeping the area clean at all times and observing the health of your orchid often.

Which Orchid Should I Start With?

As with anything, there are pros and cons. The two orchids that are recommended for beginners are the Phalaenopsis (Moth Orchid) and the Cattleya (Corsage Orchid). While both are easy to grow, there are differences between these two orchids that can help you decide which works with your schedule and environment.

Phalaenopsis Orchid

The Moth Orchid, as it is commonly known, is also a monopodial. This type of orchid has specific characteristics. It grows a single, upright stem that has leaves growing on this stem so that they are opposite of each other. The growth of this orchid is not outward but upward with age. The flowers appear at the top of the plant on a flower stalk. While there are several different types of orchids in this group, the Moth Orchid is the only one that will rebloom on an existing flower stalk. For this reason, you never cut the flower stalk of a Moth Orchid.

Now, this does not mean that the only flowers your Moth Orchid will produce come from that first flower stalk. Throughout the orchid's life, it will continue to send up new flower stalks for additional blooms. The blooms are long-lasting and come in many colors and patterns. If the conditions are right, this type of orchid will flower several times in one year.

While this is all wonderful, there are two downfalls. One is that only some varieties produce flowers that have a scent. The second downfall is that Phalaenopsis does not produce pseudobulbs. This term refers to the growth habit of sympodial orchids. But when we are talking about the Moth Orchid, the lack of pseudobulbs has nothing to do with the growth habit but the plant. Instead, it has to do with the Moth Orchid's ability to store water.

Orchids that are classified as sympodial can store water in their pseudobulbs. In the case of the Moth Orchid, this is not a possibility, which means this orchid will need to be watered more often. If you need to remember to water your plants sometimes, the Moth Orchid may not be the one for you.

But if you are looking for an early spring bloomer, then the Moth Orchid should be on your list of must-haves.

To aid you in growing the Moth Orchid, a brief monthly outline will be presented.

January and February are prime times for spike development. To do so, it is essential to start your staking process by providing ample support that will not only protect the blooms but also allow them to present themselves in the best possible way. Keep spent blooms picked up and take care when watering to reduce the chances of rot-related problems.

March and April represent the blooming season, with March being the peak time for this type of orchid. Correctly staking the spike is extremely important during this time of the year for two reasons. First, it provides support for the spike so that the weight of the flowers does not simply break it off. Staking also gives the grower the ability to show off the blooms in the best position possible by enhancing one notable feature of this orchid, which is the graceful arch. To really highlight this feature, many growers like to have the last support end at the first flower. This allows for maximum support without interfering with the natural beauty of the arch.

While there is a lot of work being done to support the flower spike during this time, one must remember that this plant is expending plenty of energy in growth and flower production. To help the orchid be the best it can be, it is essential to monitor the plant's need for moisture and fertilizer carefully. The demand for both of these limiting factors comes not only from increased growth activity but also from the fact that the days are gradually getting longer. What does this mean for the gardener? Simply put, you should expect to have to water your orchid more often.

This is an excellent time for pests to move in, and this is especially true of sucking insects. Make sure to examine your orchid closely for tell-tale signs of sooty mold and honeydew. If this is present, act accordingly to eradicate the problem before it gets too far along.

May and June are the times when all orchids of this type should be repotted or ready for potting, which refers to keikis. This type of orchid tends to be seasonal in its rooting behavior, and missing this window of opportunity creates a reproductive setback. Orchids that are repotted during this prime time of their growth cycle will have no problem reestablishing in their new home almost immediately by anchoring themselves into the fresh growing medium with new, strong roots.

Once this flush of new root growth is seen, begin regularly watering and fertilizing the plant to take advantage of this significant growing season. But stay moderate with the watering.

All the repotting should be completed in July and August. This time of year is when this type of orchid has the most growth, which means increased leaf production. The more leaves the plant produces, the more spikes the orchid can potentially make.

September and October represent a slowing down of growth. At the same time, though, inflorescence or the presence of blooms will start to appear. This is a time when the orchid should be watered less. Fertilization should also be reduced.

November and December are times to feed the orchid a "bloom-booster" type of fertilizer or one where the potassium and phosphorus numbers are higher than nitrogen, which is the 2nd and 3rd number on a fertilizer formulation. Increasing the levels of these two plant nutrients will encourage the orchid to produce the best spikes possible.

Cattleya Orchid

As one can imagine, the Cattleya orchid (Corsage Orchid) is classified as a sympodial type, which means they have pseudobulbs. These allow the orchid to store water and can survive if you miss a watering or two. They produce very showy blooms that come in a variety of bloom sizes, colors, and patterns. Many in this group enhance the beauty of their flowers with beautiful aromas. This is why this orchid's flowers are used in corsages.

While this orchid will forgive you if you forget to water them, the price one pays is a double whammy. One, the flowers are short-lived. Two, this orchid only blooms once a year, and when the flower is spent, the flower stalk will need to be removed. The Corsage orchid will produce a new flower stalk for every flowering season.

So, if you are a forgetful gardener, the Corsage Orchid is your best choice. Also, if you are looking for an orchid that will brighten your day in fall, winter, spring, and summer, this orchid is for you.

To make growing this type of orchid easier, let's take a brief look at what you will need to do in the coming months.

January and February are times when watering and fertilizing should be reduced, and dying sheaths should be removed. Staking during this time is very important because the low light of the season will cause weak spikes.

March and April are lovely months for Corsage Orchids. The winter bloomers are finishing up, and the spring bloomers are preparing to gift the gardener with beauty. This is a great time to check out the winter bloomers to see if they need to be repotted. Make sure the spring-blooming Corsage Orchids are staked.

May and June are times when the spring flowering Corsage Orchids are finishing up their display that sprung from their hardened pseudobulbs. The summer flowering types are showing buds on their soft pseudobulbs. Those orchids that are spring bloomers should be repotted now. Stake the flower spikes of the summer bloomers to keep them from breaking. Be careful with the amount of natural light the Corsage Orchid receives during this time. They have yet to get used to the more intense sunlight. To reduce the chances of sunburn, gradually expose them to brighter but filtered sunlight. Watering can be a challenge during this time due to the warmer temperatures and brighter sunlight. When in doubt, head on the drier side.

July and August are critical months for the Corsage Orchid because of temperature and growth. While your orchid is indoors, high temperatures caused by intense sunlight in a room will increase the demand for water. Since the growth happening now will affect the fall, winter, and spring bloomers, a sound fertilizer program is essential.

September and October are two months with a yin-yang nature. September is still warm in many areas, which means that the watering and fertilizing will need to be balanced according to the heat and light. One will notice, though, that as October approaches, the growth begins to show signs of slowing down. This is also a time when you should repot any Corsage Orchids that are in need.

November and December bring forth cooler temperatures along with a sun whose rays are less intense. All of these signals are forcing the orchid to slow down in its growth. What does this mean for this orchid's care? Less watering and less fertilization this does not mean no fertilization. When it comes to this orchid and the time of year, fertilization occurs less often and in a diluted form. The new growth that happened during the summer months is also changing from a green color and a soft texture to a ripening and hardening stage.

Creating an Orchid Collection

Collecting orchids is a beautiful hobby that is relaxing and inexpensive compared to other forms of entertainment. With a bit of planning, one can easily have an orchid collection that rewards the gardeners with blooms that cover close to year-round. Yes, there are a few months when little is going on in the blooming department, but in general, even a tiny orchid collection will enhance the indoor environment with colorful blooms.

Another reason to get into growing orchids is the social connection that these little beauties create. There are several orchid clubs and societies that one can join. The plus to these organizations is that they often have orchid shows where gardeners can show off their orchid successes. Participating and visiting these types of shows gives everyone an opportunity to learn more about orchid raising.

Orchid shows not only give gardeners an opportunity to show off their orchids but also give them a chance to sell and buy some. Yes, there are several sources of orchids online; an in-person opportunity gives you the chance to pick your orchids versus having your orchids picked for you. But before you go to an orchid show and get an orchid fever, let's learn what not to buy.

Plants to Avoid at an Orchid Show

Orchid selection was covered in a previous section, but that information was used to purchase plants that were not blooming. This additional information will cover orchids that are blooming, which is what you will find at orchid shows. In doing so, make sure to take into account not only the bloom health, as described below, but also the condition of the leaves and roots, as discussed previously.

While at an orchid show, it is essential to keep in mind that not everything in bloom is gold. There is a story presented in the blooms that need to be read prior to purchasing. But before we get to that, the first thing you should look at is the overall appearance of the plant. Is it perfect, or is it less than ideal? If the latter is true, then walk away. An orchid that is less than perfect represents a financial gamble. Next, pick up the plant and look for any pests, pest damage, and disease issues. Now, what is being discussed is only new problems. This is not the case. If you see any damage that can be attributed to a pest or disease issue, then stroll away.

An orchid is only as healthy as its roots, and sticking your finger in the planting medium at a grocery store or plant nursery may be fine, but it is not when one is standing at a vendor's table. But you can learn a lot about the health of the roots by looking at the top of the orchid's soil. If the top of the planting medium is fir bark, then it should still be chunky in appearance. On the other hand, if it is sphagnum moss, then it should have a springy feel. If the potting medium does not fit the bill, then you need to avoid purchasing that orchid. You could indeed repot the plant, but you are still taking a chance on an orchid whose basic foundation does not look that good.

Other observations when it comes to the orchid soil that one should be concerned about is the appearance of black algae on the soil surface along with the appearance of weeds and/or evidence of weeds being cut. Any of these observations should have you walking away from the purchase.

Avoid any orchids that show a virus color break in the flowers or streaking on the leaves.

There is another orchid product that can also be purchased at orchid flower shows, which is bare-rooted plants. As the name implies, these are orchids that have no leaves or flowers. They are simply roots. In doing so, you should take a look at the roots to make sure they are healthy. Now, anytime bare-rooted orchids are purchased, there is a process that one needs to follow prior to potting up. The first step of this process is to soak the bare roots in a bucket that contains two gallons of water and a quarter cup of cane sugar. Allow the bare-rooted orchids to soak in the mixture for 30 minutes. This process hydrates the bare roots.

After 30 minutes, lay out the roots on newspaper to dry. It is essential to keep these roots on the dry side to prevent rotting. To help with that, place the hydrated roots upright in a few clay pots. It is fine to mix with water until you begin to see new root development. Once that has happened, it is time to plant your bare-rooted orchids in their new home.

Now, sometime during your orchid journey, one will purchase a plant that brings with it pests and/or diseases. To avoid losing all your orchids to misfortune, consider isolating your new purchase from your orchid collection for a month or two. This will give you time to really study the plant to make sure there are no problems. If you think your new orchid may have a viral problem, then test it. Viral test kits are commonly available today.

V is for Vanilla

While this may seem like an odd way of introducing the next topic, the point of this approach is twofold. One is that the types of orchids run the entire length of the alphabet. The second is to draw attention to the fact that the product of a particular orchid can be found in your spice cabinet in the form of Vanilla.

There are several different types of vanilla orchids; two of the most popular cultivars of vanilla plants are Vanilla planifolia and Vanilla tahitensis. These plants are commonly called Vanilla, flat-leaf Vanilla, vanilla orchid, or West Indian Vanilla. Spanish conquistadors brought both to Europe between 1300 and 1500.

These orchids grow in a tropical environment, utilizing the rainforest's lower tree canopy as shade and support. The vines grow in a zigzag pattern that supports egg-shaped leaves. When it comes to a vanilla orchid, do not expect it to bloom immediately. It takes several years of growth before it produces a flower that can be greenish, yellow, or white. The flower only lasts a day, and the pollination window is even shorter.

In the wild, the vanilla orchid is pollinated by the Melipona bee, which is currently viewed as endangered. Due to this fact, all vanilla orchids are now hand pollinated. To complicate this issue even more, the vanilla orchid flower is only open for six to eight hours. This is significantly limiting since the pollen is also difficult to harvest, and there is only one flower per vine.

Hand pollination requires one to tear apart the flower to get to its reproductive parts quickly. Once that is done, you will find the flap, which is where the pollen is located. Using a toothpick, lift and fold back the flap to expose the male and female parts of the flower. Allow these two parts to make contact. If the contact was a success, you will know in two to three weeks.

If the bloom is not pollinated, it will fall off. If pollination is successful, the flower will remain, which means that the fruit will begin to form. Now, do not think you are going to have a fresh vanilla bean in a few weeks. It will take about six months before the bean is mature.

Care of the Vanilla Orchid

The care requirements of the vanilla orchid are the same as those of traditional orchid care, but there is one difference: the type of support. This can be a pole or trellis. The key is to make sure that this plant has something that will support its upward mobility.

Many orchid growers have an issue with watering, and the vanilla orchid is no exception. You do want to keep the planting medium evenly moist, but for this plant, it is an excellent idea to let the top two to three inches of potting medium dry out before watering.

Once you see your vanilla orchid begin to bloom, allow all the planting medium to dry out for a few weeks. To get the most out of your vanilla orchid, make sure to utilize a humidity tray and/or spray them. They require at least 85 percent humidity year-round.

Propagation of the vanilla orchid is through cuttings. This process is not complicated, but you will need to wear long sleeves and gloves. Why, you may wonder? The reason for this is a little-known fact about the vanilla orchid. Its sap can burn the skin, which is why protective clothing is required.

To take the cutting from this orchid, a knife or pruner must be cleaned and sterilized with rubbing alcohol. Next, you will need to prepare a container by cleaning and sterilizing it. Once that is done and the pot is dry, fill it with an orchid planting medium. Moisten the medium until water is seen coming out of the pot. Now, you are ready to take some cuttings.

Vanilla orchid cuttings should be six to eight inches in length. Once that is done, push the stem into the potting medium, making sure that you leave a one-inch space between the top of the planting medium and the first node. Repeat the process with all the cuttings.

Place your cuttings in the same environment as the rest of your orchid collection. Once you see a few inches of new growth appearing on your cutting, gently remove the stems to examine the root growth. If you observe white roots between three and five inches in length, then the cuttings are ready to be transplanted into individual containers. If not, place them back into the planting medium for a few more weeks.

While this process may seem a bit intimidating, the question remains: Are vanilla orchids suitable for the beginning gardener? The answer is yes, and no. A vanilla orchid is no more challenging to grow than the other orchids listed for beginners. However, pollination and production of vanilla beans are different matters. Regardless, the vanilla orchid will reward the gardener with its trailing beauty and single flower, which, with luck, will compensate the gardener with a homegrown vanilla bean.

Stay Connected with Our Gardening Community!

Thank you for reading our book! We hope you enjoyed it and found valuable insights for your gardening adventures. To keep you inspired and informed, we'd love to stay in touch.

By joining our email list, you'll receive:

🌿 Exclusive gardening tips and tricks: Directly from the experts.

💰 Special offers and discounts: On future books and gardening supplies.

📚 Early access to new releases: Be the first to know about upcoming books in our series.

🗓 Invitations to events and webinars: Join our community in learning and sharing experiences.

How to Join

Simply visit our website https://bit.ly/3R4GqCX and enter your email address, or scan the QR code below to sign up quickly!

We respect your privacy and promise not to share your information with third parties. You can unsubscribe at any time.

🌼 Happy Gardening! 🌼

Printed in Great Britain
by Amazon

56973814R00040